Christmas

by Mari C. Schuh

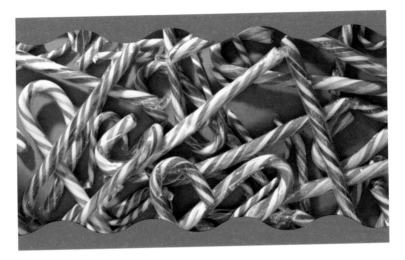

Consulting Editor: Gail Saunders-Smith, Ph.D.

Consultant: Alexa Sandmann, Ed.D.
Professor of Literacy
The University of Toledo
Member, National Council for the Social Studies

Pebble Books

an imprint of Capstone Press
Mankato, Minnesota

Pebble Books are published by Capstone Press
151 Good Counsel Drive, P.O. Box 669, Mankato, Minnesota 56002
http://www.capstone-press.com

1 2 3 4 5 6 07 06 05 04 03 02

Library of Congress Cataloging-in-Publication Data
Schuh, Mari C., 1975-
    Christmas / By Mari C. Schuh.
    p. cm.—(Holidays and celebrations)
    Includes bibliographical references and index.
    ISBN 0-7368-0979-1
    1. Christmas—Juvenile literature. [1. Christmas. 2. Holidays.]
I. Title. II. Series.
GT4985.5 .S38 2002
394.2663—dc21
                                                        00-012793

Summary: Simple text and photographs describe the history of Christmas and how
it is celebrated.

Note to Parents and Teachers

The Holidays and Celebrations series supports national social studies standards related to culture. This book describes Christmas and illustrates how it is celebrated. The photographs support early readers in understanding the text. The repetition of words and phrases helps early readers learn new words. This book also introduces early readers to subject-specific vocabulary words, which are defined in the Words to Know section. Early readers may need assistance to read some words and to use the Table of Contents, Words to Know, Read More, Internet Sites, and Index/Word List sections of the book.

10,95

Table of Contents

Christmas is on
December 25. Christians
celebrate the birth
of Jesus on this day.

Jesus was born a little more than 2,000 years ago. Christians believe that Jesus is the son of God.

Many Christians go to
church on Christmas.
They remember the birth
of Jesus. They pray
and sing.

Some people write
Christmas cards. They
wish their friends and
families a happy holiday.

Some people eat
Christmas treats. They
eat Christmas cookies,
candy, and gingerbread.

Some people decorate their homes for Christmas. They hang stockings, wreaths, and mistletoe.

Some people put Christmas trees in their homes. They hang lights and ornaments on the tree.

Some kids visit Santa Claus. They tell him what they want for Christmas.

Friends and family members give Christmas presents to each other. They share the Christmas spirit.

Words to Know

Christian—a person who follows the teachings of Jesus Christ

decorate—to add items to a room or an object to make it look nice

God—creator and ruler of the world and the universe in some religions such as Christianity

Jesus—the founder of a religion called Christianity; Christians believe that Jesus is the son of God.

mistletoe—a plant with white berries that grows on some trees

ornament—a decoration hung on a Christmas tree

Santa Claus—a jolly old man with a white beard and a red suit; Santa Claus is believed to give presents to good children during Christmas.

stocking—a covering for the foot and leg; some people hang Christmas stockings over their fireplaces; they hope that Santa Claus will fill the stockings with gifts.

Read More

Chambers, Catherine. *Christmas.* A World of Holidays. Austin, Texas: Raintree Steck-Vaughn, 1997.

Marx, David F. *Christmas.* Rookie Read-About Holidays. New York: Children's Press, 2000.

Rau, Dana Meachen. *Christmas.* A True Book. New York: Children's Press, 2000.

Internet Sites

Absolutely Christmas
http://www.geocities.com/Heartland/7134/Christmas/xmas.htm

All about Christmas for Kids and Teachers
http://www.kiddyhouse.com/Christmas

Claus.com
http://www.claus.com

Merry Christmas.com—Kids Zone
http://www.merry-christmas.com/kids_zone.htm

Index/Word List

believe, 7
birth, 5, 9
candy, 13
cards, 11
celebrate, 5
Christians, 5, 7, 9
church, 9
cookies, 13
December, 5
decorate, 15
eat, 13
family, 11, 21

friends, 11, 21
gingerbread, 13
God, 7
holiday, 11
homes, 15, 17
Jesus, 5, 7, 9
lights, 17
mistletoe, 15
ornaments, 17
people, 11, 13, 15, 17
pray, 9
presents, 21

remember, 9
Santa Claus, 19
sing, 9
spirit, 21
stockings, 15
treats, 13
tree, 17
visit, 19
wish, 11
wreaths, 15
write, 11

Word Count: 133
Early-Intervention Level: 13

Credits
Heather Kindseth, cover designer; Kia Bielke, production designer; Kimberly Danger, photo researcher

Capstone Press/Gary Sundermeyer, cover, 1, 4, 10, 12, 18
Photo Network/Myrleen Ferguson Cate, 20
Photri-Microstock, 6
Ron Chapple/FPG International LLC, 16
Susanne Thornburg, 14
Unicorn Stock Photos/Jeff Greenberg, 8